In Solace

DAXSON PUBLISHING

Praise

"Within the pages of *In Solace*, we embark on the depths of the subconscious, through a labyrinth of poetic embodiment, of the intertwining and waking moments, through a delicate balance of dreams and stark truths. Fuerte-Campos, a weaver of words which invites us to ponder our existence in its depths, in the throes of emotions which are held close, in a transformative journey through evocative prose and vivid imagery. He captivates and explores the boundless possibilities of the human psyche and the transformative journey towards understanding the complexities of his soul as well as ours. Prepare to be enchanted, enthralled, and ultimately enlightened by the mystical allure that he has set forth in his powerful words and travels through reality of both pain and acceptance."

-Estela Victoria-Cordero, Author of *Huitzilopochtli*

"Adrian Fuerte-Campos is a contemplative poet who is deeply in touch with his inner thoughts and muses over the meaning of life through the perspective of the self. This poetry collection will touch the minds of the introspective introverts and hopefully, will make us feel less alone in our time spent on earth."

-Jasmine Lan

"The poems are strong and they transmit a certain feeling of desolation."

-Maria D. Duarte

"Darkness seems unending, the pain insurmountable; Fuerte-Campos takes us on a powerful journey of transformation and healing. From the initial shock to the long journey toward acceptance and renewal, readers will find solace, understanding, & the strength to move forward."

-Crystal Reyes, Author of *Wildflower Blooming*

"In Solace by Adrian Fuerte-Campos is a powerful debut poetry collection that dives deep into themes of loneliness, self-discovery, and the search for meaning. This collection is especially important for teens, as it comes from a young author who understands and shares their experiences and emotions. The poems are raw and honest, reflecting the intense struggles and growth that are part of adolescence. With powerful language and relatable experiences, he offers an authentic exploration through challenges teens face, making this book a valuable read for young adults and those seeking connection and understanding through life's challenges."

-Wynter Eddins, author of *Afterglow*

"*In Solace* is a collection of poetry that reflects an honest truth, touching on specific time periods living life."

-Troy Legette, Author of *The Objective Scholar: Poetic Word Play*

5

In Solace

Adrian Fuerte-Campos
Foreword By: Erica B. Castro

In Solace
© 2024, Adrian Fuerte-Campos
ISBN:979-8-99005-311-3
Library of Congress Control Number: 2024908274

Cover Photo by Erica Castro
Artwork by Karime Araujo
Photography by: Erica Castro

First Edition, 2024

Printed in the United States of America

Edited by Erica Castro
Cover Design by Adrian Fuerte-Campos
Layout Design by Erica Castro

Published by: Daxson Publishing Los Angeles, Ca, 90022

Dedication

Though I understand this entire page is meant to be a space to dedicate my writing for someone else, there is no one in particular whom I wrote these words for. So I can only dedicate these words to those of you who find hope, peace, and healing through my words.

Foreword

In Solace is a collection of poems that shows the struggles, and insecurities a person experiences in trying to find their purpose in life. It paints a picture of how difficult it is to know oneself and make difficult decisions. *In Solace*, captures the emotions and feelings a person experiences in letting go of the past, trying to live in the present, and obsessing about the future. This book intertwines emotion and nature to depict the struggle that happens when discovering that life can be overwhelming, and that hope is often fleeting. Written by a high school senior, this poetry collection encapsulates the struggle a young person goes through in figuring out how to deal with the transition from adolescence to adulthood. *In Solace*, paints a picture for us to understand that the struggle is universal, and we all go through the obstacles of self-discovery and purpose. Fuerte-Campos delves into the power of fear and doubts, and how fear and doubt plague adolescent thoughts. He takes the reader on a journey of his own doubts, his struggles with the past, and his search for answers and peace. He weaves the reader into his mental health journey and the work he must do to find his way through. This collection of poems is a testament to said experience. In writing this book, it proves the power of healing through writing and finding acceptance that life is full of ups and down, but in this process of moving through there is hope at the end of the hurt.

-Erica B. Castro author of *The Pain Left Behind Surviving a Suicide Loss a Collection of Poems* and *Creating Peace through the Grieving Process*

Table of Contents

Acknowledgements

The only reason this book even exists is because of my senior-year English teacher, Ms. Lopez. She had seen that I was slacking on my work, and could see that I had not even scratched the surface of what I could do. Instead of just leaving me to rot, she presented me with an offer, an offer that helped me clear my mind, and also gave me a distraction from the things spoken about in my work. She gave me a new option that brought out my work ethic and changed the way I looked at writing. I used to hate writing as I always thought It was the textbook definition of insanity, doing the same thing over and over again. Writing letters, typing paragraphs, and making huge blobs of ink on paper, it was all meaningless to me. However, the more I have written out my thoughts, the more I have come to appreciate what writing can do for you.

Start

In dusk's embrace, where dreams are formed.
With every sunset marking a new beginning.
Each sunrise marking the end,
waiting for dusk to once again take the lead.
Each morning yawns a rhythm.
Each evening sighs a song.
With every step a path unfolds.
Each beginning marks change and chance.
Possibilities stretch out across the horizon.
Waiting on new beginnings by night, and endings by morning.
For in the medium of night skies and early mornings
I find the magic of rising new beginnings.

Everlong

Searching for myself and a purpose.
On this everlasting vacation from this purgatory,
I continue to persevere searching.
Yet each stone I overturn is yet another reason to
continue said journey.
Rediscovering who I am,
might be a journey of hardship.
Sitting here a third party in life's journey,
isolation's grip is crushing.
Here I am a part of one, I find comfort,
yet entrapment almost like a prison in that fact.
The world never rests on its everlasting journey.
Now only shadows remain where life once rested.
The heart's veins like cracks in glass
connecting what was once beating.

Letter

This is the last letter I will write to you
That you will never read.
It has been too long since the last time we spoke.
I've seen nothing, but cold winters and dark summers since.
Though no matter how much time has turned,
I cannot build the courage to send these letters.
Days turn to *Months*
Months turn to *Years*
I will continue to hold onto the memories,
yet I never allow myself to relive them.
I will continue the path I am on,
without you, only remembering.

In Solace

Under the moon's glare,
Solitude and
Tranquility rests.
Yet time itself goes to die.
Lose track of it
and yourself.
In *Solace* there is no familiarity,
there is only you.
Will you find familiarity in yourself
or will you be lost and confused?
The moon staring down.
Losing myself in its glare.
I can't even remember,
what I'm trying to forget.
There's no need for words anymore,
as silence itself has its tells.

Time

Lost in time, being a slave to it.
Waiting to see what is to come.
Sitting patiently still
waiting to discover
whether failure, success, death, life,
liberty, imprisonment, or happiness.
waits in my future.
In chains,
waiting for the passing of time
being a slave to it
is the only thing I can do.
I can only wait
I can only hope
Lost in time
I can only hope
for freedom, for life, for happiness.
I can only wait to see what is to come.

Storm

In the chilling calm of morning,
the stillness makes me cool.
The gentle breeze spilling across the sky
inspires a feeling of despair.
Pondering of what is to come,
Today? Tomorrow? The day after?
It brings a storm, a storm made of fear.
The coming storm is unpredictable, horrifying,
and near.
When the sky darkens and night falls,
the approaching storm
shakes me to my core.
Once again that fear grows.
Thunder and lighting
coming together as a pair
to *strike* down and
to give me the truth.
The storm is nigh,
and I have no clue what to do.
I will get lost in it, but maybe
that is what I have to do.

No Puedo Olvidar

Trying to erase memories,
that do no good to my mind.
I want to move on.
No matter how hard I try to do so,
the memories continue to grow
and haunt my conscience.
Laughing at me,
laughing at my perseverance,
laughing at what I've done to be rid of them.
Yet, they are still there.
All I have done has failed.
The memories are still here,
though no matter what I do,
they won't leave.

Chained

Chained to the desolate prison
that is my own mind.
I am bound by my own thoughts.
A place where fear and doubt run rampant.
Only I, myself, am able to see them and fear them.
To others, I may seem insane,
but I know what is really going on.
I know I am imprisoned.
I know I am chained.
I know I am trapped.
But, I know that there has to be a way out.
Still, I do not know what that way out is.
I want to break out.
I want to break free.
But I will continue to remain
contained
hand-cuffed
jailed
I will be stuck with this uncertainty,
until I find the damn way out.

Disappear

I wanted to vanish so completely.
That not even I would remember me.
I did not want to leave so much as a speck of dust behind.
I just want to be free.
I want to feel at peace alone.
I wish to be more alone than a desert oasis.
Surrounded by billions of grains of sand.
Once again, all I crave is to be alone.
All I crave is to be surrounded
in my own quiet depths.
I wanted to wander underneath the night's sky,
to look up at the stars, and walk under the moon's glow.
I wanted to lose myself,
to a place where only I could go.
But, after all that loneliness
what have I accomplished?
This feeling was new,
a new emptiness had become of me.
This new feeling of being alone.
This wasn't like any feeling from before.
This was different.
This was horrifying.
I was comfortable being lonely.

Lost

Lost, I cannot find my way in this labyrinth.
Each wall in this maze is a memory I long wish to forget.
Memories of sorrow or joy,
all of them part of the past.
I turn each corner searching.
Searching for a key to free me from this place.
This never ending maze of visions,
I long wish to abandon.
I am a prisoner of my own volition,
trapped in memories of my own hesitations,
and regrets.
Though I am in this maze of my own will,
I cannot let myself out.
I must remember my failures,
or I will be doomed to repeat them.

Gone

Today, I am just me.
Who am I?
I must build upon who I am now.
I can not piece together who I was,
but now I must search and hope.
Whoever I was is gone.
As I strive to remember,
I keep falling and failing.
I look in the mirror and I see nothing familiar.
Who am I?
Am I a son? Am I a friend? Am I a good person?
It has been so long since,
I could recollect who or what I am.
I often feel as if I, myself, am no one.
I don't know who I am anymore.

Autumn

Orange leaves falling from trees,
leaving them behind.
Like people leave their pasts behind.
The leaves like memories of a forgotten past
rotting on the ground, waiting to disappear.
Falling to the ground.
In their respective shades of gold,
their stories lie on the floor, untold.
The trees, barren and empty, yet free.
Though each leaf is forgotten, they remain.
Watching them dance as they fall,
through the autumn air.
Hearing the crunch below my feet,
as I step on each leaf.
I forget another memory.

Trapped

Wondering where I am.
Ensnared in this prison,
I am searching for salvation.
A hope of finding an escape to this void.
In the distance I see a flame,
a flame of hope.
Consumed of the shame of self doubt,
I begin the trek to the light.
I'm doubting if I'll ever reach it.
All I can see is a distant light,
a light so far.
Where am I?
With no exit and no entrance,
Cut off from everything else
trapped, in a room.

Rock Climbing

Climbing this mountain with no end in sight,
each rock I climb, another memory replayed.
With each crack in the cliff, a trap.
Waiting for me to grip that stone,
and fall to my own failure.
I have to avoid those failures,
no matter the cost.
With each memory played,
my future is increasingly safer.
Each rock is a memory of pain,
forcing me to remember my past.
With each memory conquered,
the less likely I am to repeat it.
Rock climbing is a sport
of self-improvement
in climbing and in mind.

Dark

In a room absent of light,
nothing but darkness.
Pitch black, surrounding me.
Finally after spending an unknown amount of time,
finally a light appears.
Being without a light has starved me for it,
reluctant to approach it for fear of being burnt.
I approach the light, appreciating its warmth,
But am met with nothing, but a burning fire.
Burning me beyond recognition.
Once again returning to that room,
absent of light.
Once again scouring the darkness for a light,
but wishing for one that won't burn me.

Confusion

I find myself in the middle of the street,
with a thick fog surrounding me.
Dazed and confused, as to what is going on.
I'm lost, yet I feel familiarity with my surroundings.
I don't know what is coming for me.
Not knowing what is coming
is causing fog to grow in my heart.
Each passing moment,
I am growing more lost.
Is this feeling all that
I will experience in the near future?
This feeling of being lost in life.
Will it be all that consumes me?
Or will I find a way, in this familiar dream?
Will I find a way out of the fog?

Just One

Just a *bad day* has evolved.
Day after day
week after week
I'm tired of this never ending feeling of despair.
Month after month
year after year
Just a *bad day*?
Lying to myself, finally coming to realize
that it hasn't been just a *bad day*,
It has been a very long time since I felt glee.
Despair and sorrow have become a daily part of me.
With no end in sight of this unending feeling.
I have no hope of finally being let out of this cycle.
I am left to continue,
and begin the same dreaded day over again.

Cut

Seeing the blade on the floor caked in blood.
The air around reeks of rusted iron.
Stepping into the puddles of red along the floor,
as it seeps into the cracks of the tile.
Red liquid all over the floor.
Tears mixed in along with it.
I try to walk towards the source,
but a glass pane holds me back.
I try to crack the glass, but it does me no good.
Stuck pounding on it to try and break through.
Forced to watch the blood and tears leak out.
Forced to stand by and watch,
binded with these jaded feelings of uselessness,
not able to lend a hand.

Thunder

The raw clap waking me out of my sleep,
ripping me out of the nightmare I was in.
Waking me up from the fear of what is to come.
Thunderous roars shaking the ground,
creating cracks and crevices in my room.
Letting fear and disappointment seep into my heart.
Drowning in the feelings of despair.
Unable to breathe,
and unable to keep going.
With another thunderous strike,
I awake once again in my bed.
Still struck with fear and despair
from the nightmare the thunder ripped me out of.

Missing Something

Wandering the streets,
pleased with the gloomy weather.
Left with a feeling of incompletion,
missing something at my hip, and in my head.
Feeling this emptiness, I am lost.
I am confused with no clue what to do.
Though I search my pockets,
I cannot find out what is missing.
The memory of what or who has eluded me.
Wandering the streets alone once again.
The gloomy weather keeping my mood in good spirits.
It won't let me down,
like that missing thing did.

Conflict

To find a new beginning.
I will sift through the mud and ground.
Accepting that this war is lost,
clears my fear and doubts.
Though my heart wants to clear the skies of all the fog,
my mind knows I need to accept the chaos.
Shall I follow what my heart wants,
or what my mind knows I need?
In search of a light.
If I have to,
I will drag myself along the jagged ground.
Confusion is all I find.
Leaving me for dead.
Wandering no man's land.
Itmo is tearing my peace,
and tranquility to shreds.
Doubt and fear claim their victory.
I've long since surrendered.
Searching for a white flag to raise
Searching for an end to this chaos
Every morning, evening, and night
conflict wages in my mind.

The Fog

A son lost.
A father found.
Wandering the clouded city they called home,
searching for a part of them that is missing.
A part of them that they have longed for.
A part of them that connected both
the father and son together as one.
Without that part, they are lost and confused as can be.
Searching through the fog in their hearts,
hoping to once again be reunited with that missing piece.
That piece that binds them together.
When they finally encounter that piece,
it is not the same.
It is also lost to the fog,
Together they are lost once again.

Listening

Everytime I close my eyes,
and listen to what is around me.
All I hear is cars roaring by,
loud yelling, and metal hitting the floor.
Pure chaos is all I hear.
To try and calm it, I stop listening.
I open my eyes, and all I see is me.
By myself again,
once again I close my eyes.
Trying to escape what I see,
just to get right back to the chaos.
Right back into the absurdity that I hear,
to the loud and distracting noise.
Once again wishing to open my eyes.
Trapped going back and forth,
never able to rest in one place.

Crawl

Trying to make my way home,
gravel embedded in my skin,
pebbles cutting my knees,
and stones slicing my hands.
This unbearable weight holding me down,
forcing me to scratch and claw at the ground.
Forcing me to crawl to make it home.
I cannot send strength to my legs,
without sacrificing the strength in my mind.
I need my mind to remain absolute
and remain as strong as I can.
To make it home,
to make it home,
to peace and tranquility.

Walking in the Rain

Each raindrop another distraction.
The continuous sound of water droplets,
calming beyond words.
The rain is a place of peace and tranquility,
each puddle and droplet a distraction.
A distraction from my own despair,
a welcome distraction at that.
The constant sound of rain hitting the floor,
like the stones that crash against one another,
in the receding waves at the beach.
Walking in puddles,
feeling the drops of water.
Feeling them hit my head and shoulders,
makes my head quiet down.
It makes all the memories fade for just a moment.
It lets me appreciate them for what they are.
Instead of punishing myself for remembering them.
I love walking in the rain.
It makes me feel
like myself.

Pushing

Pushing forward through the day.
More of a struggle than I ever thought it would be.
Doing the best I possibly can.
Pushing myself up the mountain.
Burning myself along the way just to make it through.
Cutting myself on the sharp ground,
slicing open my hands
and knees pushing forward.
No matter how far I make it,
something always seems to make me fall
back down to the bottom.
Just to once again start my day over again.
Pushing myself up this mountain daily.

Purpose

Searching for a purpose,
in this land of turmoil we call America.
Pushing all of the noise aside,
sifting through all the chaos.
Searching for a purpose
putting out a bounty on meaning.
Chasing dreams that just get in my way.
Chasing meaning like no other.
Making my way through this endless labyrinth of life.
Searching for a purpose
with a heart built on hope.
But a mind obsessed with truth and reality.
I must continue my search
for a purpose, and for peace.

Weights

Racking another weight to clear the clouds in my mind.
The heavy clanking and scraping of metal,
helps to clear my head of thoughts.
It helps to only focus on pushing that weight.
Only focusing on the weight falling upon my chest,
only focusing on dropping that weight off my chest,
and back onto the rack.
With each weight, with each scrape,
with each clank, and with each rack
lies peace, and tranquility.
Once I re-rack that weight,
my mind is refilled with intrusive thoughts.
The only way to remove that mold from my mind,
is to put on more weight and unrack it.
Once again, only focused on throwing that weight off my body.
Constantly lifting and re-racking the weight.
The sharp sounds of metal scraping
quiets my mind, more than before.
Without the noise, I am stuck.
Forced to reconcile with the words in my head.

Experience

My past experiences have taught me,
like a teacher explains to a class how to do math problems.
Except these problems are all up to me to solve,
but with no help it is pointless.
I am left to bear these issues,
and have no idea what to do.
With each predicament comes another feeling of responsibility,
a responsibility to hold onto all of this guilt and disdain.
This burden tears at me.
It rips and lacerates my conscious.
Taking me down another peg somehow,
even though I feel as if I am at rock bottom.
The power of remembering what has happened
still continues to haunt me.

Doing Me

Everyday I wake up,
I continue to do me.
Focusing on myself,
working on myself to do the best I can.
Trying to become a new person,
yet still retain who I am.
With each waking moment
I feel as if I am drifting away from who I used to be.
But with change comes doubt.
Maintaining my drive to do better,
I take one step at a time to better myself.
With each step I take,
I fear that I will slip,
and make a fool of myself.
For what will all of this progress bear?
What was all of this effort for,
all of this change?
It is for me.

Sleep

Sitting in bed dreaming,
that in another world
I can escape the noise.
All of the chaos residing in my head.
Hoping in that other world that I find silence.
Wishing that I can finally do what I've only dreamt of.
Trusting that in that other world
I can find the peace to start anew.
Wanting to start my own venture.
Thrown out of my sleep
only to wake up,
and face reality.
Forced to stare up at my debacles
while they tower over me.
Wishing to escape into another dream.

Broke Free

In shadow's depth,
chains envelop.
I was once bound,
now I strive to grow.
Wishing for freedom's guiding light.
Snapping free from old bonds.
Embracing the truths made apparent to me.
Switching between joy and pain.
Free from fear's cuff-links.
With every step a new opportunity and creation.
testifying to the joy of freedom.

Skipping Stones

Skipping stones on the river bank.
Each skip a challenge to overcome.
Each skip a hardship already triumphed over.
Blindly hoping for a chance at another skip,
but that's the beauty of it.
Once the stone sinks,
another stone is to be thrown.
Each skip a challenge to overcome,
Each skip a hardship already triumphed over.
Waiting to see how many skips you can get,
challenging yourself.
To skip that stone as much as you can,
challenging yourself to be a better you.
But always remembering who you are.

Last Stretch

In the day surrounded in light,
Just over the horizon, it's in view.
The coming darkness of uncertainty and concern.
The fading light, a silent friend.
It hints at the nearing end.
Memories glistening in the fading light.
Slowly turning to dust as the light leaves it.
With the receding light,
a tender solace, and fleeting grace.
For accepting the end is the true beauty.
And accepting the new start,
is the ultimate medicine for a
broken soul.

Burn

In the hours before dawn,
Where aspirations and dreams grow,
A soul burns with determination and willpower.
Waiting to be released from the cage that holds it from greatness.
Through hardships and obstacles come terror and distrust.
Overcoming said daunting hurdles,
Requires the chains to be snapped and set aside.
With relentless determination and unwavering focus,
The souls flame burns as strong as ever.
Through lows and highs, the goal remains the same.
Days turn to weeks, and weeks to years.
Each a trophy to show the mountains overcame.

Leave

In the shadowed corners of memories,
my heart struggles with an ultimatum.
To leave behind what I once held dear,
or brave the path of fear and doubts.
A bond turned frayed and torn.
Farewells whispered with a lowered tone.
The disappointment and grief of letting go,
The nostalgia ripping at me.
All chaos in my mind in the moon's embrace.
Abandoning what I once held near and dear,
causing an ache deep in my gut to awake.
But now I must continue this journey,
putting that itch to the side
to focus on what is to come.

Guided

In silent depths where darkness roams,
a heart learns to accept its situation.
Among life's twists and turns,
tranquility can be reached and mastered.
Acceptance leads the race in the mind,
embracing flaws and imperfections.
There is no winning or losing,
only finding peace amidst the chaos.
Through hardships,
you will find the correct path.
Transforming the dark in your life into light,
releasing regrets, and letting go of the past.
Let acceptance guide your path,
and guide you to your true destiny.

On the Path

When I close my eyes,
I can only see the path I am on.
Surrounded by an endless stream of trees,
on a never ending dirt path, following signs.
It's dark outside,
I can only see what is in front of me.
I can't see what's ahead of me,
yet I remember what I left behind.
I will continue to follow this trail,
not knowing where I will end up.
But being hopeful,
I get to where I am meant to be.
I, continuing to follow this path, blindly.
I take another step.
Blindly hoping it is not a cliff
I could fall off of.
Blindly hoping it is solid ground.
Hoping this path will take me
where I am meant to be.

Ocean's Glare

Here I am
standing in the sand
with grains between my feet.
Grains all over my towel, and all over my face.
I stand here, still, admiring the ocean's glare.
Wondering why the ocean is so tranquil.
Is it the sounds of the waves crashing against one another?
Is it the sounds of the sea gulls passing over me?
Is it the sounds of the rocks clacking together on the shore?
Or is it the silence they all create when they come together?
Put them all together,
and all I can hear is them.
The peaceful sound of the beach calms me,
but also it frustrates me.
Because the only way I can find this peace,
is here standing in the sand
with grains between my feet.

Free

I have freed myself,
from the confines of my own mind.
Free from all the memories
I made myself remember.
Free.
But have I really escaped my memories,
or have I just replaced them,
with memories of loneliness,
memories of solitude,
memories of isolation.
I have freed myself of my memories.
Memories filled with joy and happiness.
I have forced myself to forget,
what I have treasured most.
Now I have filled that void with,
memories of failure and fear.
Am I really free?

Aftermath

During the chaos of the storm,
I struggle to find myself.
But calm myself knowing,
the stillness will return.
The storm just needs to pass.
Everything surrounding me
is chaotic and destructive.
Yet I wait, and wait, and wait.
When will the storm end?
When it ends,
I will sit in its aftermath,
trying to find myself.
I will find a sense of resilience and peace.
For finding the difference between calm and storm,
is the beauty and reward of persevering
through the fear of what is to come.

End

Beginnings cannot be without an ending.
Endings brings about beginnings,
but that is the way it will always be.
The cycle begins, yet also ends.
Endings bring about a new space for beginnings.
Yet, in the night it is all that is to be seen,
and all that it is to be heard.
The end sweet yet sour.
It decays in the air.
Each farewell ticks down the clock until it arrives.
Silent, yet loud, it is deafening.
Nothing left but stars and darkness,
the end is nigh.
The sun is snuffed out.
The end arrives,
as the curtains unveil.
Surrounded by darkness,
and words of dismissal.

56

Epilogue

Writing these words has given me time to reflect on my thoughts and the incessant ideas that plague them. I believe that I have grown and have learned more about myself throughout the process of writing these pieces. I hope that those of you reading my work can relate and can do some growing yourselves. I had kept myself sane throughout the long process by remembering that I was not in this process alone, I remembered that someone was helping me and guiding me along the entire process. My teacher, Ms. Lopez, has been a constant reminder to myself to continue writing and not give up. She has reminded me that there is someone counting on me, and that there are people who I didn't want to disappoint. Nonetheless, I feel as if this project has helped me grow, and get past some things that have been weighing me down in life. I hope that those of you who have read my work, relate to my words, and make these changes yourself. I also hope that some of you take the challenge of writing yourself out of hurt, pain, and confusion.

58

Author Bio

Adrian Fuerte is a high school student making his way through his senior year, class of 2024. He mostly keeps to himself, but is trying to change, not only the way he goes about his daily life, but possibly change the outcome of his future. He is trying his best to navigate through life and find his way. He is trying new things, and this book is one of them. He feels as if maybe trying new things might give him a new outlook on life. He understands that this line he is tip-toeing on is one of the things people struggle with the most in their own lives, and he wants to try to give them the same opportunity he is trying to create for himself. Hoping through his words people find peace and know they are not alone

Publishers Note

Daxson publishing was created to help marginalized artists publish their work, so the world can hear their voice. The vision for this publishing house is to help people get their work out there, and not have them struggle finding their way through the publishing process. Everyone's voice deserves to be heard, and we are here to help. If you are interested in submitting a manuscript, email daxsonpublishing@gmail.com.